The
Chocolate Chip Challah
Activity Book

written and illustrated by
Lisa Rauchwerger

An Interactive Guide
to the Winter, Spring
and Summer Holidays

BOOK 2

UAHC PRESS • New York

To my father,

whose curiosity, creativity, and resourcefulness

has been an inspiration and a blessing.

Acknowledgments

My thanks and undying gratitude to Judy Kummer, Carie Carter, and my Imzadi, Kaila Schwartz, for your wise counsel and suggestions in preparing this book. Thanks also to Misha, Robin Holzman, and Yael Crawford for finding and suggesting new activities to share and for providing helpful source material. A big thank-you hug to Rabbi Judy Kummer's class as well as to Janice Leitner, Ileen Gross, Robin Holzman, and Carie Carter for testing the activities for me. Thank you, Mom, for your unending support and guidance and invaluable teaching experience. To Rabbi Hara Person, thank you for your keen yet gentle guidance and inordinate patience when it looked as if this would never get done, thank you to Bryna Fischer for expert copy-editing, and thank you Ken Gesser and Stu Benick for continuing to believe in me. Last but not least, thanks to Michelle Young and Rick Abrams for your honest enthusiasm in promoting my work. I couldn't have done it without you!

Introduction

Welcome to the whimsical world of smiling veggies and interactive holiday experiences. In these books you will find holiday projects and puzzles for the whole family and the whole class. There are activities to do with a parent or adult, and activities to do alone. Many of these activities lend themselves to family education programs as well. These books are meant to be used in connection with *Chocolate Chip Challah: An Interactive Family Cookbook.* Ideally, these activity books should be used to supplement the cookbook—as another way to "do Jewish," at home or in the classroom.

The activity books follow the format of the cookbook, traveling through the Jewish year and stopping to explore each holiday through informative and fun activities. The activities were devised to be teaching tools as well as enjoyable diversions. They teach valuable lessons in *teshuvah, tzedakah, gimilut chasidim,* and other important Jewish values.

These books were meant to be aids in healing the world, not contributors to its destruction. Thus, I have attempted to use materials that are edible, recyclable, or easily re-usable. To make some of the word-related activities and puzzles reusable, cover the relevant pages with clear contact paper and use dry-erase markers.

To use these books you will have to use your creativity and your imagination. Through making your own challah cover, decorating bags of food for the hungry, and planting seeds for future Jewish rituals, you are becoming God's partner in Creation. May you continue to grow in wisdom and good deeds, "doing Jewish" and, in the process, helping to repair the world.

Go forth and make memories!

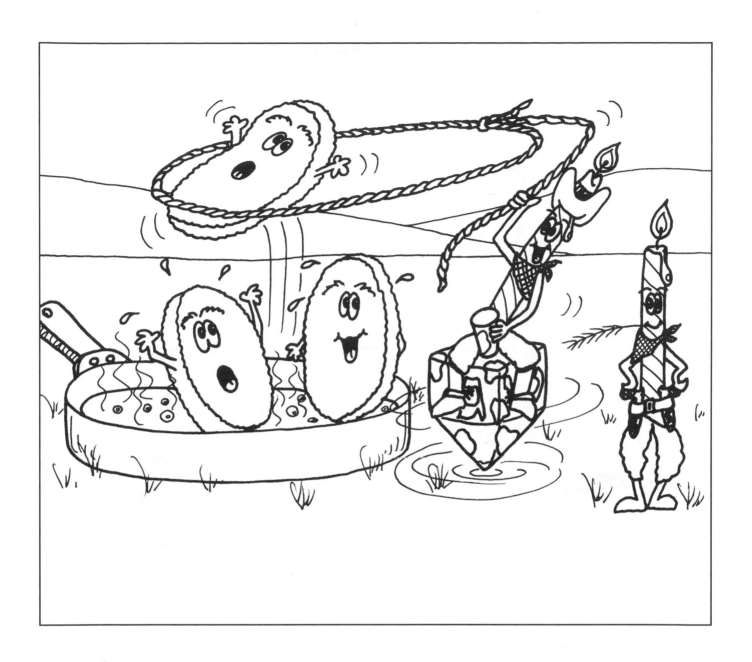

Chanukah

Chanukah, the "Feast of Rededication" and "Festival of Lights," celebrates the victory of a small band of Jews over the great Greco-Syrian army in 165 B.C.E. It is also a day to recall the story of the miracle of the oil (for the menorah in the Temple) that should have only lasted for one day but instead lasted for eight days. We commemorate this miracle by eating foods fried in oil, such as potato latkes and jelly doughnuts (in Israel), and we celebrate Chanukah for eight days and nights to remind us of the miracles that happened so long ago.

Chanukah Vocabulary

Chanukah: Literally, "dedication"; the "Feast of Rededication" or "Festival of Lights" that celebrates the victory of a small band of Jews over the Greco-Syrian army in 165 B.C.E. and their fight for religious freedom

Chanukiah: A nine-branched candelabra, or candleholder, used on Chanukah

Gelt: Money, sometimes in candy form, given to children on Chanukah for eating and playing dreidel

Hellenists: Those Jews who wanted to be like the Greeks, or who followed the Greek ways

Judah: Mattathias's oldest son, who led the band of Maccabees to victory

Latkes: Potato pancakes fried in oil; usually eaten by Ashkenazic Jews on Chanukah

Maccabees: Meaning "hammers," the small group of Jewish rebels led by Mattathias who fought and defeated the Greco-Syrian army in 165 B.C.E.

Menorah: A seven-branched candelabra, or candleholder, used in the Temple in Jerusalem.

Larry Latke and Sasha Sufgania play a game of dreidel.

Interactive Paper Dreidel Chain

Make your own Chanukah decorations. Cut out colorful dreidels, put them together, and then complete the sentences below, writing your answers on the sides of the dreidels. Write each set of answers on a different dreidel. String up the dreidels and you'll have Chanukah decorations that are unique to your family. Go forth and make memories!

What You'll Need
colored paper or cardstock
scissors
a stapler
a single-hole punch
string, ribbon, or thread

What to Do
1. **Trace** dreidel template onto another sheet of paper and **cut out**.
2. **Trace around** it 2 times onto colored paper to make 2 dreidels.
3. **Cut out** both dreidels (they can each be a different color).
4. **Fold** each in half lengthwise along dotted line.
5. **Place** them on top of each other so the sides fold up, away from each other.
6. **Staple** the two together along the fold.
7. **Push out** the sides so you have a 3-D dreidel.
8. **Make** seven more like this, in different colors.
9. **Punch** a hole in each top for the string.
10. **Complete** the sentences below, then **write** each sentence and its answers on a dreidel.
11. **String** them up and **enjoy!**

Suggestions
- If your family has four or fewer members, each person can write on one side.
- Put your names and the date at the bottom so you can remember from year to year who said what.
- Answer one question each night for eight nights, or answer all eight questions the first night.
- Make a new chain each year, even each night!
- Come up with your own questions, or write different answers to the same questions each year.

INTERACTIVE DREIDEL QUESTIONS:

Fill in the blank with the appropriate word, then complete the sentence:

_____ is part of our family when we . . .

1. Togetherness	**5.** Fun
2. Learning	**6.** Love
3. Mitzvah	**7.** Sharing
4. Tradition	**8.** Celebration

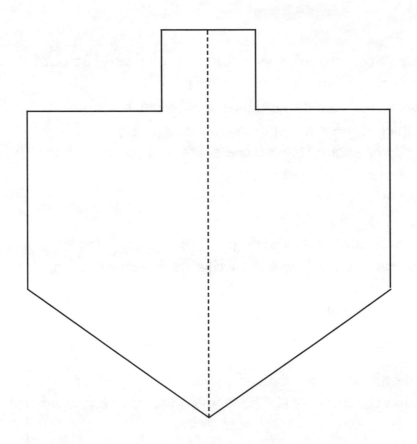

Chanukah Finger Puppets

Act out your own Chanukah finger play, using the characters below. Color and cut out the ones provided, or make your own. This is a good activity for older children to do with their younger siblings. Let the show begin!

What You'll Need

crayons, markers, or colored pencils
scissors
tape or small pieces of hook-and-loop fasteners
blank paper and pencil (optional)

What to Do

1. **Color** the characters on each puppet.
2. If you wish to make your own, **trace** the shape of the blank one onto another sheet of paper and **draw** your own character/s.
3. **Cut out** the puppets with scissors.
4. **Attach** a piece of rolled tape or hook-and-loop fastener to one side of one tab, then **roll** the puppet around your finger and **tape** or **fasten** it closed.
5. **Act out** the Chanukah story in your own way!

Suggestions

To trace, place a blank sheet of paper over the pattern, hold the two pages up to a window, and then trace the outline onto the new piece of paper.

ANTIOCHUS

IDOL

MACCABEE

GREEK SOLDIER

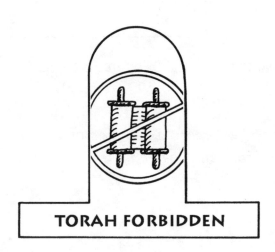

TORAH FORBIDDEN

TEMPLE DESECRATED

MIRACLE OF OIL

12

Chanukah Stamp Placemat

Make a colorful placemat that you can use the whole week of Chanukah.

What You'll Need
colored pencils, markers, or crayons
scissors
access to a laminating machine (any copy store)

What to Do
1. **Copy** the page if you need more than one placemat.
2. **Color** the stamp.
3. If using the copy in the book, carefully **tear** the page out of the book, and trim edge with scissors.
4. **Laminate** it. Now you have your own Chanukah placemat!

Tu Bishvat

Tu Bishvat is the New Year of the Trees. Its name means "the fifteenth day of [the month of] Shevat." On this holiday we celebrate the first signs of spring in Israel, where trees are just beginning to show their new buds, even though in North America it is still winter. We can celebrate Tu Bishvat by planting trees, either here in our communities or in Israel. In this book you'll get a chance to meet a tree, and you'll plant your own parsley for Pesach!

Tu Bishvat Vocabulary

Adama: Hebrew for "earth"

Eitz: Hebrew for "tree"

Eitz Chayim: "Tree of life," sometimes referring to the Torah or to wisdom, from the Torah service

Fifteen fruits: The custom of eating fifteen different kinds of fruit on Tu Bishvat because it falls on the fifteenth day of the month

Pri: Hebrew for "fruit," as in the blessing "borei pri ha-eitz," "Creator of the fruit of the tree"

Tu Bishvat: Literally, "fifteenth day of the month of Shevat," the holiday known as the "New Year or Birthday of the Trees," which comes just as trees are beginning to bud in Israel

Tu Bishvat seder: The ancient mystics modeled the Tu Bishvat seder after the Pesach seder, in order to study, taste, and celebrate the fruit of the tree at the beginning of spring in Israel. It involves four cups of wine, usually of different colors, to represent the changing seasons. With every cup a different group of fruit is offered and tasted. The four cups also symbolize four different stages in our relationship to God.

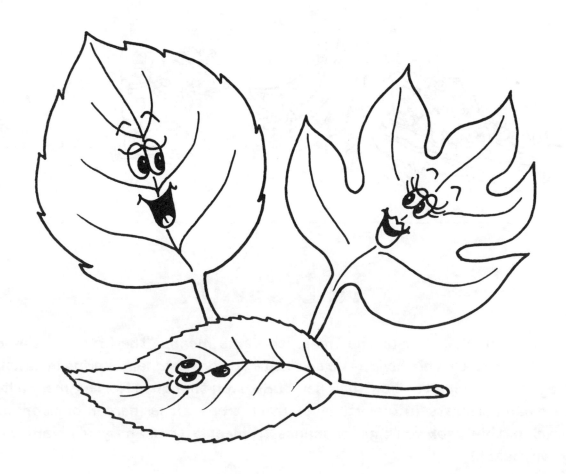

Tu Bishvat Word Search

```
T O N C B R Q E T R E W O L F Q R T
S R E P L T A I L U F O B H T E Z E
T V E A I R F T G H B J K C T O Z M
O J A E O U A Z A K I R U A D Y R R
A V E I B N X C F N R E W A I J O E
S E A H N K R H E Q T P B T M A H D
H T L Y R A K A B Y H A C I L H E E
C H I E A L H Y A E D R L I O S F S
E W A U I C L I V R A K P A G A Q T
I S J F R A J M A I Y E M U E L N A
A H T M V F A U Z B A R I L Y D C V
C A B E I R S V M J E A R T H U T H
E N L H A M A D A N Z A E T A R L S
T A O M U I S X I Y E T O U S A B I
A D S F E Y L H G E W G M K E I A B
L Y S A A P S H E Y T K Y A I N V U
K J O I L N W N A L E Y A X E U K T
R W M P U R C A F E Z S E Q O P L A
A J L S E Y O T U B I S H V A T W O
B E A G A L E V I D H E G A P T K I
S P O A D E H B R A N C H E N I R P
```

Find the following words and phrases in the puzzle above. Words can be up, down, backward, forward, or diagonal. NOTE: There are no spaces between words and no apostrophes in the puzzle. For example, TU BISHVAT will look like this: TUBISHVAT.

TREE
PRI
EARTH
TU BISHVAT
FRUITS
RAIN
OXYGEN
EITZ CHAYIM
BIRTHDAY
SOIL

TU BISHVAT SEDER
ADAMAH
SUNSHINE
WATER
BARK
LEAF
BRANCH
TRUNK
FLOWER
BLOSSOM

(see page 74 for answers)

Meet a Tree

Since Tu Bishvat is all about trees, this game will give you the opportunity to get to know a real tree in your area. IT SHOULD BE DONE WITH ADULT SUPERVISION. This activity is taken and adapted, with permission of the author, from Joseph Cornell, *Sharing Nature With Children*, 20th anniversary ed. (Nevada City, Calif.: Dawn Publications, 1998), p. 28.

What You'll Need
2 or more people, 4 years old and up
blindfolds
a forest, grove, or park with access to trees

What to Do (ADULTS SHOULD READ THROUGH BEFORE DOING)

1. **Pair off.**

2. **Blindfold** your partner and **lead** him or her through the forest, grove, or park to any tree that attracts you. (How far will depend on your partner's age and ability to orient himself or herself. For all but very young children, a distance of twenty to thirty yards usually isn't too far.)

3. **Help** the "blind" child to explore the tree and to feel its uniqueness. Specific suggestions work best. For example, if you tell children, *"Feel the tree,"* they won't respond with as much interest as if you say, *"Rub your cheek on the bark."* Possible questions include: *Is this tree alive? Can you put your arms around it? Is the tree older than you are? Can you find plants growing on it? Are there any signs of animals? What shape are the leaves? How do they feel?*

4. When your partner is finished exploring, **lead** him or her back to where you began, but take an indirect route. Remove the blindfold and let the child try to find the tree. Suddenly, as the child searches for *his or her* tree, what was a forest becomes a collection of very individual trees.

JOSEPH CORNELL'S NOTE: A tree can be an unforgettable experience in a child's life. Many times children have come back to me a year after we played *Meet a Tree* and have literally dragged me out to the forest to say, "See! Here's my tree!"

Plant Parsley for Pesach

Plant parsley during Tu Bishvat, and you'll have it for your seder table at Pesach!

What You'll Need
a packet of parsley seeds, either Italian (flat leaf) or curly parsley
a small paper cup or small clay or peat pot
potting soil
water

What to do
NOTE: To promote germination, **soak** seeds overnight in warm water before planting.

1. **Fill** your cup or pot with potting soil.
2. **Follow** the instructions on the back of your seed packet.
   a) **Place** seeds in cup and **cover** lightly with soil.
   b) **Water** to keep soil evenly moist until seeds sprout, approximately two to four weeks, depending on soil and weather conditions.
   c) For best results, **keep** at a temperature of 65–75° F. Keep pot in a dark place until seeds sprout, then **place** in a sunny spot.

Suggestions
- Pick a time each day to check your seeds and see if they need watering.
- Make sure they get sunlight and don't dry out.
- Tend your seeds carefully, and you'll be able to have your very own parsley for Pesach!

Purim

On Purim we read from the Book of Esther. The book tells the tale of our people's escape from destruction at the hands of evil Haman, prime minister of ancient Persia, and relates the bravery of Queen Esther and her cousin Mordechai. It is called *Purim,* meaning "lots," because Haman drew lots to determine on which day the Jews would be killed. The story is handwritten on a scroll, or *megillah,* which is like a Torah scroll but has a roller on only one side. Purim is a holiday on which we are expressly commanded to be happy. And nothing makes people happier than cookies! It is traditional to deliver treats to friends and relatives during this time. In this chapter you will be able to make your own basket to hold these treats. You'll also get to decorate a Purim Potato Head, create your own *gragger* (noisemaker), and fill in a funny version of the *megillah.* Be happy, it's Adar!

Purim Vocabulary

Ad d'lo yadah: Aramaic phrase for "until you don't know" (the difference between blessed Mordechai and cursed Haman)

Adar: Hebrew month in which Purim is celebrated on the fourteenth and fifteenth days

Ahashuerus: King of ancient Persia

Esther: Jew, cousin of Mordechai and future queen

Gragger: Noisemaker used to drown out Haman's name; *ra'ashan* in Hebrew

Hadassah: Literally, "myrtle tree"; Esther's Hebrew name

Haman: Evil prime minister who wanted to kill all the Jews

Hamantashen: Three-cornered fruit or nut-filled cookies

Matanot l'evyonim: Hebrew phrase for "gifts to the poor"; one of the mitzvot associated with Purim

Megillah: Otherwise known as the Scroll of Esther; A hand-written scroll from which we read the story of Purim

Mordechai: Esther's brave cousin and Jewish hero

Purim: "Feast of Lots," from the Hebrew word *pur*, meaning "lot"

Purim shpiel: An often-humorous play poking fun at the Purim story

Shalach manot: Gift baskets of food and treats brought to friends on Purim. Also called *mishloach manot* in Hebrew and *shalach manos* in Yiddish; one of the mitzvot associated with Purim.

Shushan: Capital city of ancient kingdom of Persia

Shushan Purim: The day on which those in Jerusalem (and other walled cities) celebrate Purim

Vashti: Spunky first Queen who refused to submit to King's demands

Zeresh: Haman's wife

Purim Puzzle Hints

Here are some vocabulary words to learn that will help you solve this puzzle. You might also want to look at a *megillah*, or Scroll of Esther, to find the answers.

Amalek: evil ancestor of Haman

Banquet: a large, fancy meal; a feast

Cubits: an ancient type of measurement

Hodu: land in ancient Persian kingdom

Kush: land in ancient Persian kingdom

Poppy seed: original flavor of hamantashen

Provinces: the parts of a country outside of the capital

Scepter: a wand carried by a monarch as a symbol of power

Taanit Esther: Fast of Esther

Zeresh: Haman's wife

Purim Puzzle

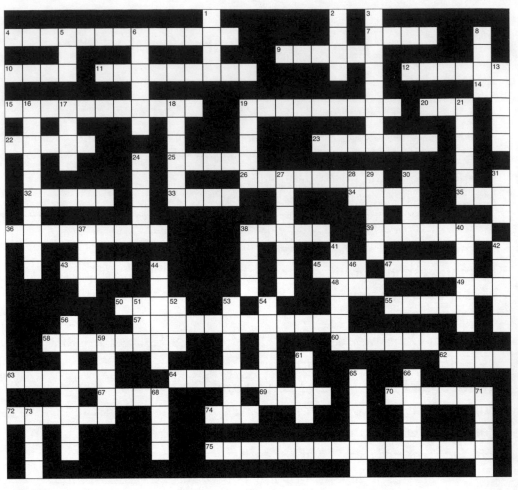

ACROSS

4 Shabbat prior to Purim
9 King Ahashuerus lived in this land
7 _____ the megillah
10 Wipe out (H's name)
11 Esther's brave cousin
12 Festive meal (Hebrew)
14 Jewish Renewal word for God
15 3-cornered cookies
19 Purim treat, original flavor
20 Haman's cap
22 Evil prime minister
23 Capital, ancient Persia
25 King's chamberlain
26 Scroll of Esther
32 Esther = daughter of Mordy's _____
33 King A gave this to Haman, then to Mordy
34 Ancient Persian kingdom stretched from _____ to Kush
35 # of feasts Esther prepared
36 127 _____ in King A's kingdom
38 Goofy
39 Purim play
43 No eating allowed
45 Pleasure
47 Banquet
48 Mordy wouldn't do this to Haman
49 Female pronoun
50 Fret
55 Another Purim cookie flavor
57 Purim care packages (in Hebrew)
58 Fancy feasts
60 Form of ancient book
62 "Tra-la-la-la..."
63 Kind to animals
64 Meaning of Esther's Hebrew name
67 Wicked
68 Queen's hubby
70 Esther won this contest
72 A mensch
74 Mordechai was one
75 "Gifts to the poor" (in Hebrew)

DOWN

1 Munch
2 Disguise for the eyes
3 Purim noisemakers
5 A gamble
6 Haman's wife's name
8 Theater production
13 "Be _____, it's Adar!"
16 King of Ancient Persia
17 Purim celebrated on the 14th of _____
18 Jewish Queen
19 "Feast of Lots"
21 Fast (in Hebrew)
24 Graggers make a lot of this
27 Haman wanted Mordy to die on the _____
28 Doctors make you say it
29 Mordechai rode on one
30 Ancient Persian kingdo stretched from Hodu to _____
31 Whose name never appears in the Megillah?

37 Where Shushan is today
38 Haman had 10 of these
40 Jewess, Mordy's cousin
41 Gallows built 50 _____ high
42 King's women/wives
44 Spunky 1st Queen to King A
46 Terrible twos' favorite word
51 Utilize
52 ____, T E T, U I U, V O V, W U W
53 King's golden stick
54 Evil ancestor of Haman
56 Esther's Hebrew name
59 King's life partner
61 Bad way to die
62 Pouch
66 "Oh, today we'll _____(x2) be"
68 At full volume
71 Purim treats taste _____
72 Haman had pointed _____

(see page 74 for answers)

Recyclable Popcorn Gragger

Noisemakers, also called *graggers* or *ra'ashanim*, are used in synagogue to drown out the name of Haman when we read from the *megillah* on Purim. You can make your own *gragger* out of recyclable materials in just a few easy steps. It makes a beautiful sound and is loud enough to drown out the loudest *megillah* reader! And when you're done, you can recycle the bottle and make the popcorn for a snack!

NOTE: A glass bottle makes the nicest sound, but for younger children, a plastic bottle works just as well.

What You'll Need
½ to 1 cup of uncooked popcorn kernels
    (depending on the size of your bottle)
a small glass (or plastic) bottle with a long neck,
    like a soft drink bottle or small grape juice bottle
    Make sure the bottle has a cap that closes tightly
a sheet of paper
colored tissue paper or construction paper (optional)
markers (optional)
glue or tape (optional)

What to Do
1. **Fill** the bottle about halfway with popcorn kernels. To make it easier to get all the kernels into the small opening, **roll up** a piece of paper into a funnel and **tape** it closed. **Put** the small end of the funnel into the bottle, then **pour** the kernels into the bottle.
2. **Put** the cap on the bottle and tighten. **Turn** it upside down, **hold** the neck of the bottle, and **shake!** How does it sound? **Adjust** the amount of popcorn until your *gragger* sounds the way you like it.
3. If you want to decorate the bottle, you can **tape** or **glue** pieces of colored paper onto the bottle—just **remove** the paper before you recycle the bottle.

Ad-Lib Megillah

What to Do
1. One person **reads** the clues under each line; another person **provides** the answers (without looking at the text.)
2. **Take turns** filling in the blanks for a fun twist on Megillat Esther.

NOTE: If you cover the pages with clear contact paper before beginning, you'll be able to create as many versions as you wish.

Now it came to pass in the days of King Ahashuerus who reigned in the capital city of Shushan, that the king made a _____ feast for

adjective

all the _____ of the land. Vashti, the queen, made a feast for all

plural noun

the women. After _____ days of partying, when the king was very

number

_____, he sent for his queen, to show off her _____

adjective   noun

before all his guests. But Queen Vashti refused to _____ before

action verb

the king. As you might guess, the king was quite miffed. The king's

advisors told him to find another _____ who would be more

noun

_____. So the king held a contest to choose the fairest

adjective

_____ in all the land to be his new queen. And we're still not sure

noun

what happened to poor Vashti.

Meanwhile, back in town, there lived a certain _____ named

noun

Mordechai. He had a niece (or was it his cousin?) named Esther, whose

Hebrew name was Hadassah. When the news of the _____

kind of contest

contest reached them, Esther, being a fair maiden, was brought to the palace. Her uncle (or was that cousin?) Mordechai asked her not to reveal her Jewish identity to the king. Esther was _____ and

adjective

gracious and impressed the head servant of the women. The king was also _____ impressed with Esther and loved her more than all

adverb

the other fair young _____. He put the royal crown upon her

plural noun

_____ and made her queen instead of Vashti. Then the king, who

body part

loved to party, made a _____ feast in honor of his new queen.

adjective

Meanwhile, lurking in the shadows at the gates of the palace, two of the king's chamberlains plotted to _____ the king. And who

nasty verb

just happened to be passing by but our hero Mordechai, who overheard the _____ plot and saved the king! _____! The two cham-

adjective _exclamation_

berlains were_____, and the event was recorded in the

nasty verb (past tense)

Book of Chronicles for the kingdom's _____ record.

adjective

After _____, the king set one of his nobles, Haman the

amount of time

Aggagite, above all his other royal _____, and made all the king's

plural noun

subjects bow down to Haman. But Mordechai the Jew refused to bow down before _____ Haman. Mordechai did this not once, not

adjective

twice, but _____ times, and it was Haman's turn to be miffed.

large number

Haman was told that Mordechai was a Jew and that was why he refused to bow down (because Jews don't bow to anyone but God), and

Haman hated all the Jews because of what Mordechai had done. Haman convinced the king (without mentioning names) that this people should be destroyed. So King Ahashuerus put Haman in charge of the _____ deed. And Haman held a lottery to determine on
nasty adjective

what day the _____ would take place. They cast lots (*purim* in
type of event

Hebrew) and the lot fell on the thirteenth day of the month of Adar. The king's scribes sent out a decree to all the _____ in the kingdom,
plural noun

announcing that on that day, the Jews were to be destroyed.

When Mordechai heard the news, he put on clothes of mourning and cried out loud before the palace gate. And throughout the city and in every _____, there was much weeping, _____, and fasting
noun ... *verb ending in "ing"*

among the Jews.

Meanwhile, back in the palace, Esther heard what was about to happen to her people and sent a _____ to Mordechai to
type of communication

get the details. Mordechai sent a message back informing her of Haman's plot to kill the Jews. He urged Esther to _____ to the
action verb

king and plead with him to save her people. Esther told him that it was very dangerous for someone to try to see the king if he or she had not been called. Unless the king extended his golden _____ to the
noun

person, the penalty was death. Mordechai warned Esther that even though she was queen, her life would not be spared if her people perished. Maybe this was the reason she had become queen.

Esther asked all the Jews of Shushan to fast for her for three days and _____ nights. On the third day she put on her most
number

_____ clothes and went to stand in the entryway of the king's
adjective

throne room. The king sat on his royal _____ and in his
noun

_____ was his golden _____. King Ahashuerus looked up,
body part   noun

saw Esther standing there, and extended his _____ to her.
noun

Esther approached the king, and he asked her what she wanted. He told her he would grant her up to _____ his kingdom. Esther asked him to
fraction

come to a _____ banquet and to bring Haman. The king was
adjective

_____ and called _____ Haman to hurry up and get ready
adjective   adjective

for the party.

Haman was excited to be with the "in" crowd at the palace, but was still angry about Mordechai. So he decided to build a gallows to hang Mordechai. Meanwhile, back at the palace late that night, the king was_____ and couldn't sleep, so he called for his _____ to
adjective   noun

read to him from the Book of _____. As he was dozing off, he
plural noun

heard the account of how the guards plotted to kill the king and of how Mordechai had saved his life. King Ahashuerus asked what _____
noun

Mordechai had gotten for this _____ service, and was told that
                                    adjective
nothing had been done.

Just then, _____! Haman stopped by, and the king asked him,
              interjection
"What shall be done for the _____ whom the king desires to
                                  noun
honor?" Haman, thinking the king was referring to him, said, "Dress this

man in _____ robes, and place a royal crown upon this man's
          adjective
_____, and sit him upon the king's _____, and lead him
  body part   *animal*
through the streets of Shushan calling out before him, 'This is what is

done for the _____ whom the king desires to honor!'" Then the
                noun
king said, "Excellent! Hurry up and do all this for Mordechai, the Jew!"

"Curses, foiled again!", thought Haman.

Soon after, Haman was whisked off to another _____
                                                     noun
prepared by Esther. The king and Haman enjoyed the feast until the king

again asked Esther, "What is your request? Up to _____ my
                                                    fraction
kingdom will I grant you." Esther replied, "If it pleases you, let my

_____ be spared and my people, too, for we are to be destroyed!"
  noun
The king asked, "Who is this _____, and where is he who would do
                                noun
this thing?" Esther cried, "The enemy of my people is this _____
                                                          nasty adjective
Haman!" The king was furious, and he stomped out of the room in a

rage. He ordered that Haman be hung on the _____ originally
                                                noun

made for Mordechai. King Ahashuerus put Mordechai in charge of all of Haman's _____. And the king felt much better. (It's good to be
                                    plural noun
the king!)

King Ahashuerus set Mordechai above all his _____ in place of
                                              plural noun
Haman, and decreed that all Jews _____ his land could defend
                                  preposition
themselves on the day they were to be _____. Mordechai
                                       verb (past tense)
sent the king's _____ messengers throughout (the)
                adjective ending in "est"
_____ to spread the news. And the Jews rose up and defended
large area
themselves on that day, the 13th day of Adar. And Mordechai proposed
that the 14th and 15th days of Adar become days of feasting and
celebration, (a) _____ of sending packages of _____ to
                 amount of time   _plural noun_
friends and _____ to the poor. And they all lived happily ever after
            plural noun
(well, most of them!).

Purim Potato Head or Shushan Squash

Use the assorted props on the next page or draw your own to create a variety of Purim characters on a potato or squash! When you're through playing, you can use the vegetable in one of the recipes in *Chocolate Chip Challah!* Have fun!

What You'll Need
at least one potato or squash
thumbtacks or tape
crayons, markers, or colored pencils
scissors

What to Do
1. **Color** the props on the following pages, or **draw** your own on a separate sheet.
2. **Cut out** the props.
3. Using tacks or rolled pieces of tape, **attach** the props to a potato or squash to make different combinations of Purim faces and characters. **Act out** the story and **change** the faces as you go, or **use** a different vegetable for each character. **Use** your imagination, and have fun!

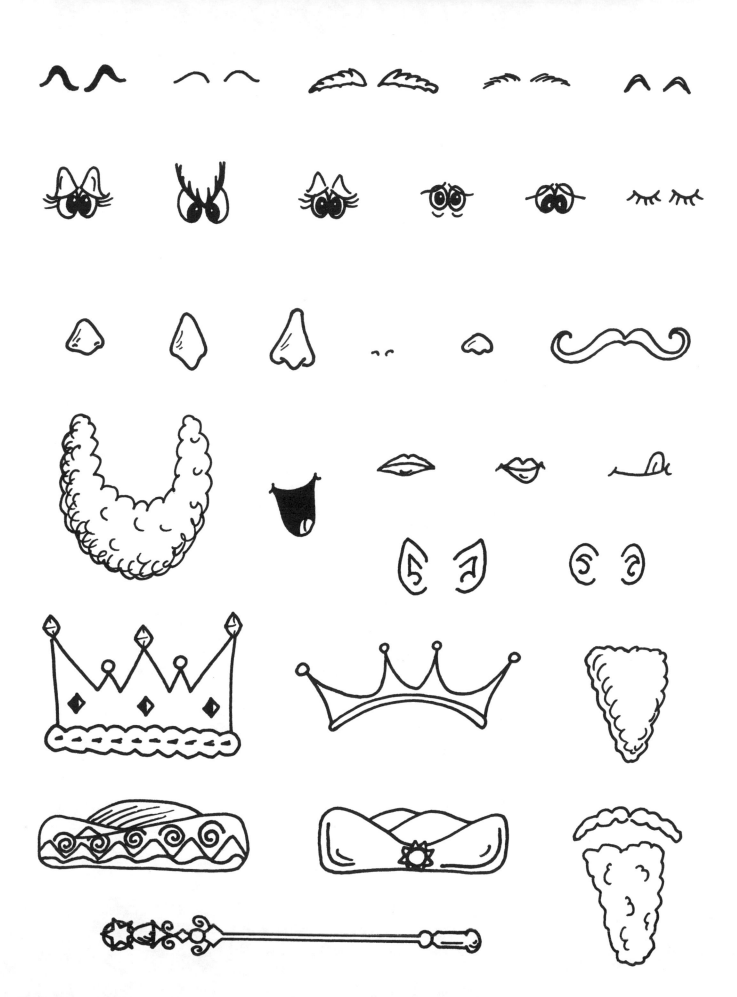

Pretzel Shalach Manot Basket

Did you make tons of yummy hamantashen but have no place to put them? Now you can make a pretzel basket and deliver them to your friends and family! This recipe is from *Nikki and David Goldbeck's American Wholefoods Cuisine*, 1983 edition, pg. 351.

What You'll Need
¾ c. warm water (110° F)
1 T. (1 packet) active dry yeast
1 t. honey
2 T. oil
1 t. salt
about 1¾ c. flour
1 egg yolk and 1 t. water (for basting)
½ t. coarse salt (optional)
extra flour for board

Utensils
large mixing bowl
measuring cups and spoons
mixing spoon
knife
dish cloth
pastry brush
small metal bowl, approxiately
    3 inches high and 5 inches across
12 x 12-inch piece of aluminum foil
baking sheet

What to Do
1. **Combine** water, yeast, and honey in a large mixing bowl and **let stand** for about 10 minutes until dissolved and bubbly. **Add** oil, salt, and as much of the flour to the yeast as necessary to form a dough that can be kneaded.
2. **Turn out** onto a floured work surface and **knead**, adding flour as necessary, for 8 to 10 minutes. When dough is no longer sticky, **place** it in a bowl and **cover** it with a clean dish towel. **Let** the dough **rise** in a warm place for 45 minutes. Then **punch** it down and **divide** it into two balls; **let** it **rest** for 8 to 10 minutes, to make it easier to roll.
3. **Separate** dough into balls approximately the size of limes and **roll out** each one with your hands into a long thin cord. **Place** the cord on the piece of aluminum foil. **Repeat** with each ball of dough, **placing** cords parallel to one another until you have at least six, then **switch** directions and **start laying** the cords across the others.
4. **Start to weave** them, beginning at the center and working your way out.

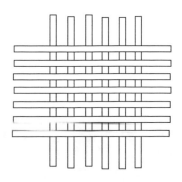

5. When you have used all the dough, carefully **lift** the aluminum foil with the braids, and **place** over the upside down metal bowl. **Trim off** the dough that hangs over the edge. **Roll** this leftover dough into a ball and **form** into two cords. **Twist** them together. This will be the rim of your basket.

6. **Attach** the twisted cord to the ends of your basket, using a little water to stick them together. You can also **weave** the ends of the cords into the twisted piece, attaching them that way. When everything is all braided together, **cover** the basket with a dish towel and **let rise** in a warm place for 45 minutes.

7. Near the end of the second rising, **preheat** the oven to 425° F. **Mix** egg with water and **paint** on surface of basket. **Sprinkle** with course salt if desired.

8. **Place** basket (still on bowl) on a baking sheet and **bake** in the oven for about 15 minutes, or until braids start to turn golden brown. **Remove** from oven carefully (have a grown-up do this part) with potholders and carefully **peel off** the foil from the basket. **Turn over** the basket and **paint** the inside with the egg mixture. **Place** the basket back on the baking sheet right side up without the bowl this time, and **bake** another 10 to 15 minutes, until the inside gets a little brown. If the edges start to brown faster than the rest, **cover** them with strips of foil.

9. **Remove** basket and **cool** on a wire rack. **Eat** within a day for best taste.

1)

PRETZEL BASKET, UPSIDE DOWN
(FIRST BAKING)

2)

PRETZEL BASKET, RIGHT SIDE UP
(SECOND BAKING)

Pesach

Pesach is the holiday of rebirth, of spring, of freedom and of matzah. It is a week-long festival commemorating the Israelites' Exodus from Egypt and the beginning of political freedom for a people who had been slaves for 400 years. The Hebrew word *pasach* means "passing over." When God sent the ten plagues on the Egyptians, God spared the Hebrews, *passing over* them, so we call this holiday *Pesach*, or Passover. On Pesach we eat dry, unleavened bread called matzah, and we eat no foods made with grain or leavening. All the food we do not eat is called *chametz*. We clean our homes extra carefully to get rid of any trace of *chametz*. In the following pages, you will get to sing and write some funny Pesach songs, make your own matzah, and have a chance to get rid of your spiritual and emotional *chametz*.

Pesach Vocabulary

Betzah: A roasted egg, symbolizing rebirth and renewal

Charoset: A sweet mixture of apples, nuts, and cinnamon (or other sweet dried fruit and spices) that symbolizes the mortar used in the making of bricks for Pharaoh

Chatzeret: Romaine lettuce, usually bitter, symbolizing the bitterness of slavery

Dayenu: It would have been enough"; said and sung at the point during the Pesach seder when we praise God for all the miraculous things God has done for us

Elijah: The prophet who is supposed to appear and herald the coming of the messiah. We leave a cup of wine and a place at the table for Elijah, and even open the door for him during the seder, just in case.

Haggadah: The book we use to tell the story of the Exodus and to keep everything in order

Karpas: A green vegetable, usually parsley, symbolizing spring and renewal

Ma Nishtanah Halailah Hazeh Mikol Haleilot?: Hebrew for "Why is this night different from all other nights?"

Maror: Bitter herb, usually horseradish, symbolizing the bitterness of slavery

Matzah: "Bread of affliction"; the dry, flat, unleavened bread Jews eat on Pesach to remind us of our hasty departure from Egypt and the affliction of slavery

Miriam: Prophetess and sister of Moses. She led the people in song and dance at the shores of the Red Sea; according to the midrash, she also brought a traveling well of water to the people in the desert.

Moses: Hebrew leader, prophet, and lawgiver who led the Israelites out of Egypt and through the desert to Mount Sinai to receive the Ten Commandments

Pesach: Passover, from the word *pasach* meaning "passing over"; the holiday commemorating the Israelites' Exodus from Egypt and the beginning of their political freedom; also the roasted shank bone (or, in vegetarian seders, the beet) representing the blood put on the doorways so that the Angel of Death would "pass over" the Israelites' houses

Pharaoh: King of Egypt during the Exodus

Seder: Literally, "order"; the ceremonial meal on Pesach during which we eat special foods, sing songs, ask certain questions, and tell the story of our Exodus, all in a specific order

Chametz Cards

On Pesach we try to get rid of the *chametz*, the leavening in our houses. We clean our homes from top to bottom; we empty our cabinets, cars, and pockets of all traces of *chametz*; and then we have a special ritual burning of the last of the crumbs. But Pesach is also a time to get rid of the *chametz* in our lives, to let go of some of the things that are puffing us up and keeping us from being the people we want to be. These things can be physical, emotional, or spiritual, but the important thing is to recognize them and make an effort to get rid of them in the coming year.

What to Do

1. **Write** some of the things you would like to get rid of on these Chametz Cards.

2. **Cut** them out with scissors, **crumple** them up, and **dump** them in a container to recycle.

You are now *chametz* free! How does it feel?

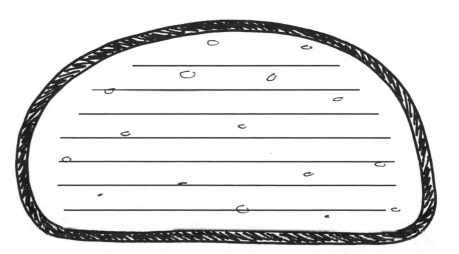

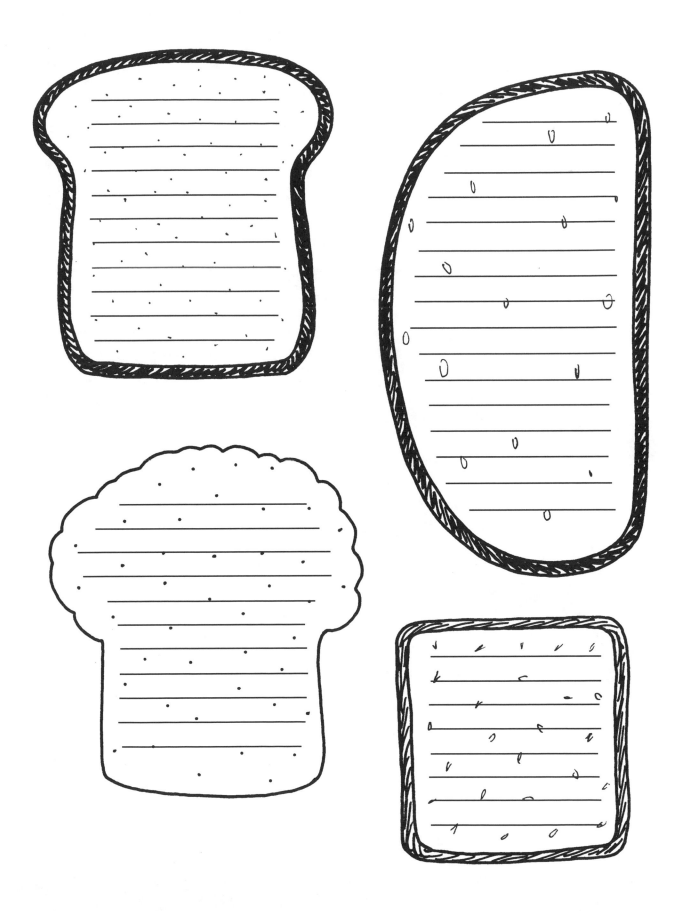

Silly Pesach Songs

The *Haggadah* teaches us that we should feel as if we ourselves personally went out of Egypt. The following are silly Pesach songs that will help you relive the experience. A friend and I came up with these songs for our creative Pesach seder, but feel free to write your own! Take a favorite song, one that you know well, and write your own lyrics (words) to it. Then try it out at your seder!

I've Been Workin' on the Pyramids

(Sung to the tune of "I've Been Workin' on the Railroad")
Lyrics by Lisa Rauchwerger and Carie Carter © 1999

_____

I've been workin' on the pyramids,
All the live long day.
I've been workin' on the pyramids,
I wish Pharaoh would go away!

CHORUS:
Can't you hear the whips a-crackin'?
Oy! How they make us slave!
Schlepping stones and stamping mortar,
For a day of rest we crave, OY!

Oy! Vey! Vat ve gonna do?
Oy va voy, see the bruises on you-hoo
Oy! Vey! Vat ve gonna do?
Maybe I'll become a Jew!

Someone's in the palace with Pharaoh!
Someone called Moses, I know-o-o-oh!
Is he gonna help us get out-ta here?
I think it's time to go.

I'm so tired of the pyramids,
Sand in my hair and toes.
How I wish we could get outa here,
I could finally clear my nose! (CHORUS)
(Oy! Vey! . . .)

I've been watchin' Pharaoh's palace,
See how he lives so fine.
While we're slavin' on the pyramids,
Not allowed a sip of wine.
(CHORUS)
(Oy! Vey! . . .)

Oy! It's hot and dry in Egypt,
Here in the land of Goshen.
Even the camels are a cravin'
Just a dab of water or lotion!
(CHORUS)
(Oy! Vey! . . .)

In Through the Sea

(Sung to the tune of "Under the Sea," from *The Little Mermaid*)
Lyrics by Lisa Rauchwerger ©1999

Moses pleading with the people to leave Egypt:

The slavery is always harder
In somebody else's tent.
You dreamed about leaving Egypt,
So it's about time you went.
Just look at the world around you,
How could you put up with more?
Such awful conditions for you;
What more are you waiting for?

In through the sea, in through the sea,
Life will get better, once we get wetter,
In through the sea.

In Egypt land, you work all day,
Out in the sun you slave away,
Then Pharaoh's daughter found me in the
water, Down by the sea.

As slaves in Egypt you're moping,
As off to the pyramids you go.
But if you were free you'd rejoice,
For if you were free you'd know.
'Cuz when you have freedom you can
Do so many wondrous things,
No worrryin' 'bout what Pharaoh will do, just
Wonderin' what tomorrow brings! (Oh yeah!)

In through the sea, in through the sea,
No one will beat you, whip you and treat you
Hor-ri-bl-y!

I know you're used to all the work,
but I gotta tell ya', Pharaoh's a jerk!
Life will be nicer, if I can entice-yer,
In through the sea (in through the sea),
In through the sea (in through the sea),
Since life is hard here,
we've got to leave here natural-ly (naturally)

Even my sister and my bro,
they're all packed up and ready to go.
So pack up your bread dough,
we've got to scram, tho',
In through the sea.

The blood caused a flood,
The frogs fell like logs,
The lice big as mice,
The beasts would not cease,
The cows they're dead now,
The boils on the goils,
The hail it did wail so loud! OY!

Locusts ate the crusts,
The dark in the park,
The firstborn forlorn,
The cries in the dark,
The plague passed us by,
We all heaved a sigh,
And oh how Pharaoh wailed! OY!

In through the sea, in through the sea,
Pharaoh will let us, he will not get us,
Leave it to me!

What's Egypt got, a lot of sand?
We've got our Miriam and her band!
Even your camel know how to jam-el,
In through the sea.

Take your pajamas, don't forget the llamas,
In through the sea.

Go pack your timbrels,
and your brass cymbals,
It'll be better, once we get wetter,
Ya', we in luck here, outta da muck here,
In through the sea!

Humorous Pesach Headlines

The following two pages contain mini-newspapers telling the story of the Exodus from Egypt and the Israelites' journey to Mount Sinai. Use them like the Ad-Lib Megillah on page 26 and fill in the blanks for a very funny look at the Pesach story.

What to Do

1. One person **calls out** the types of words needed; another person **provides** the answers without looking at the text.
2. **Take turns** coming up with words, then **read** it out loud together. Have fun!

NOTE: If you cover the pages with clear contact paper before beginning, you'll be able to create as many versions as you wish.

The Raamses Review
Vol. I—Special Slavery Edition

PHARAOH ORDERS HEBREW SONS KILLED

In a(n) _____ act to save
adjective
his kingdom from _____,
plural noun
Pharaoh ordered that all new-
born Hebrew sons be thrown
into the Nile. Hardware store
owners say that sales of
water wings, _____,
hardware store item
and pitch have gone through
the roof! Census takers have
noticed that despite the
decree, Hebrew children are
continuing to be born at a(n)
_____ rate.
adjective

REBELLIOUS MIDWIVES SAVE HEBREW BOYS

Shifra and Pua,
Midwives to
the Hebrews, have been
defying the decree of
Pharaoh and are continuing
to bring _____ boys
adjective
into the world, sources say.
So far, they have not been
punished.

PLAGUES DEVASTATE COUNTRYSIDE

All of Egypt has been suffering from one
_____ plague after another.
For _____ days Egyptian citizens have
number
found _____ in their drinking
plural noun
cups, _____ in their beds and
animal (plural)
_____ on their _____!
plural noun   body part (plural)
Sources at the palace say that ex-prince
Moses claims these _____
adjective
plagues will end if Pharaoh lets the
Israelites go, but Pharaoh's magicians
are not so sure.

KING'S NO. 1 SON DIES

Pharaoh's firstborn son, _____,
a funny boy's name
heir to all of Pharaoh's _____
plural noun
has been killed by the tenth plague to
attack this city. Sources close to the
palace say that the Israelite exodus is
near at hand.

HEBREW SLAVES PREPARE TO LEAVE

Israelite slaves are packing all their
_____ and preparing to leave
plural noun
town ASAP. Laundromats and luggage
stores are doing a booming business!

The Hebrew Times
Vol. II—Special Exodus Edition

All the news
Moses lets
us print

EXODUS
FROM
EGYPT!

MIRACLE ON REED STREET!

Hebrews Flee Pharaoh's Chariots

In a(n) _____ act of faith, a
adjective
mixed multitude followed Moses
out of Egypt, pursued by _____
number
of Pharaoh's men riding his _____
adjective ending in "est"
chariots.
Unfortunately for Pharaoh, nobody
returned to Egypt. Who will build
the _____ for him now?
plural noun
Inquiring minds want to know!

Moses Leads Masses Through on Dry Land—Gives God credit—Then Asks for Day Off!

Our brave and fearless leader
Moses, _____ and
adjective
_____ from his trek
adjective
through the Red Sea, was overheard to have said, "Oy, am I tired!"
and immediately put in a request
for some time off. Fortunately for
us, but unfortunately for Moses,
God refused.

Nachshon Takes First Step Toward Freedom; WATERS PART!

Rumor has it that the waters of the
_____ Sea did not part until
color
Nachshon ben Aminadav dipped
his _____ into the waves
body part
and walked into the water until it
almost covered his _____!
body part
A medal of honor will be presented
to Nachshon at the next
_____ stop, as soon as the
noun
_____ blacksmith can find where he
packed his anvil!

Miriam Organizes Women's Music Festival at Sea Shore; Women Dance 'til Dawn

Our prophetess and #1 song leader
Miriam led a group of _____ at the
plural noun
in singing and _____. A _____
verb, ending in "ing"   adjective
shores of the sea. A _____
band was started with Miriam on
timbrel and Yocheved playing the
_____. Even the camels
musical instrument
were jamming!

The Shofar

Vol. IV—Special Redemption Edition

Freak Thunderstorm to Blast Mountain

Out of nowhere, a(n) _____ (adjective) thunderstorm will blast Mt. Sinai, weather forcasters predict. Clear skies will give way to loud, _____ (adjective) thunder, unexplained fire and smoke and _____ (adjective) shofar blasts. Stay tuned to your local _____ (noun) weather channel for more up-to-date forcasts.

MOSES DISAPPEARS FOR 40 DAYS
NATIVES GET RESTLESS

According to a(n) _____ (adjective) source, Moses was last seen fixing his _____ (noun) strap on his way up Mt. Sinai. He hasn't been seen since. _____ (p ural noun) left behind are beginning to worry, especially the Jewish _____ (plural noun) in the crowd...and that would be...you guessed it...almost everybody! Some say he will _____ (verb) any day now. But some have forgotten him already and are beginning to cause a little trouble with big brother Aaron.

MOSES RECEIVES 2 TABLETS OF LAW!

Moses, our brave and _____ (adjective) leader, has handed down a new set of _____ (plural noun) and commandments from God for us to follow. No wonder he was up there for so long, can you imagine chiseling it all out of _____ (noun) ?! Oy, so many _____ (plural noun) little time! What was #9 again?

Aaron Bows to Pressure—Builds Golden Calf

_____ (adjective, past tense) by Moses' absence, Aaron agreed to _____ (action verb, infinitive) an idol for the _____ (plural noun) at the bottom of the mountain. According to rumor, the women refused to donate their _____ (plural noun) and were rewarded with the holiday of Rosh Chodesh.

The Schlepper's Weekly

Vol. III—Special Wandering Edition

Sick of Manna, Hebrews Pine for Raamses Pita Palace & King Tut Hut

Remember the _____ (adjective) 'ole days? static crackle static: "Hi! Welcome-to-Raamses-Pita-Palace-may-I-help-you?" Yes, I'd like a _____ (adjective) combo-meal with a # _____ (number) side of pita chips and a diet papyrus pop, oh, and can you put a few _____ (adjective) tehini packets in with that order please? Whatdayamean you don't have any more _____ (desert animal) sauce?!

MOSES REFUSES DIRECTIONS—WE KEEP WANDERING

According to a(n) _____ (adjective) source, Miriam claims she offered to take a group of _____ (p ural noun) from the Israelite hiking club on a tiyul (trip) to the local Beduin-run AAA office to request a map of the Sinai and neighboring _____ (geographic areas,) , but her brother refused to even consider the idea, saying, "If God had wanted us to _____ (verb) , God would have provided a map."

IF ONLY THERE WERE SCALLIONS...

A(n) _____ (adjective) group of _____ (noun or plural noun) schleppers are starting to complain about the food in the desert. "At least in Egypt we had _____ (fast food, plural) and _____ scallions," some complained. Breath mint sellers are also very unhappy.

Miriam Dies—WHERE'S THE WATER?

The sad news of Miriam's death was immediately followed by a(n) _____ (adjective) discovery—the wells which have followed us in our travels have disappeared! No one can figure out where the _____ (p ural noun) have gone or how we can find our _____ (noun) in the desert without _____ (verb) . All supplies of freeze-dried H_2O are used up and we haven't passed a Beduin in-tent swimming pool since we left Egypt. _____ (noun) experts are working on the problem.

Make Your Own Matzah

NOTE: This is a project to do only with an adult. Make sure you get permission to use the kitchen, and have an adult with you when you do this recipe.

Experience the "bread of affliction" firsthand by making your very own matzah! Go on, how long could it take? The whole point is to do it quickly, as if you were leaving Egypt now! Matzah that is "kosher for Pesach" is watched the whole time it is made, from the time the wheat is planted until the time it comes out of the oven, to make sure nothing goes wrong during the process. If the wheat or flour ferments or goes bad, it cannot be used. There are special places where you can watch them make matzah, but now you can do it in your own home! May your fingers be swift!

What You'll Need

3¼ cups whole wheat flour   fork
1 cup cold water   baking sheet
mixing spoon   wire cooling rack
big bowl   spatula
rolling pin

What to Do

1. **Preheat** oven to very hot (425°–500°).
2. **Mix up** the dough in a large bowl. Now **take** a small piece of dough and **knead** it for 90 seconds. Now quickly **roll out** the kneaded dough on a clean, flat surface with a floured rolling pin. **Roll** it into a thin circle. **Poke** holes in the circle of dough with a fork. **Repeat** steps a few times until you have enough to fill a baking sheet. Make sure the dough doesn't get wet or dirty, because then it won't be kosher.
3. **Place** the matzot carefully onto a baking sheet, and **bake** in a very hot oven until it starts to get light brown, NO LONGER THAN 10 MINUTES. (Let an adult put it in the oven for you.) **Watch** the dough the whole time it is baking.
4. **Remove** the baking sheet from the oven with pot holders (this is a job for an adult), and **let** the matzah **cool** on a wire rack.
5. **Now sample** your creation! What does it look like? What does it taste like? What sounds does it make when you eat it? They don't call it the "bread of affliction" for nothing! Welcome to the desert!

Yom haAtzmaut

Yom haAtzmaut, besides being a tongue twister, is Israeli Independence Day, the day Jews celebrate regaining our independence and becoming a free people in the Land of Israel. On May 14, 1948, the State of Israel was born. On Yom haAtzmaut, we celebrate by dancing, waving Israeli flags, and singing Jewish songs. On this day, in Israel and in America, people celebrate by going on picnics and barbeques, and eating Israeli foods like felafel and Israeli salad. In this chapter you'll have a chance to try your luck at an Israel crossword puzzle (if you get stuck, check your cookbook), prepare your own hummus, and make birthday wishes for Israel. Happy Independence Day!

Yom HaAtzmaut Vocabulary

Felafel: Popular food in Israel, made of ground chick peas shaped into balls, fried in oil, and stuffed in a pita with salad

Kachol V'lavan: Hebrew for "blue and white," the colors of the State of Israel; also a song

Yerushalayim Shel Zahav: "Jerusalem of Gold," a song written by Naomi Shemer; also refers to the way light glints off Jerusalem stone, making it look golden

Yom haAtzmaut: Israeli Independence Day

Israel Crossword Puzzle

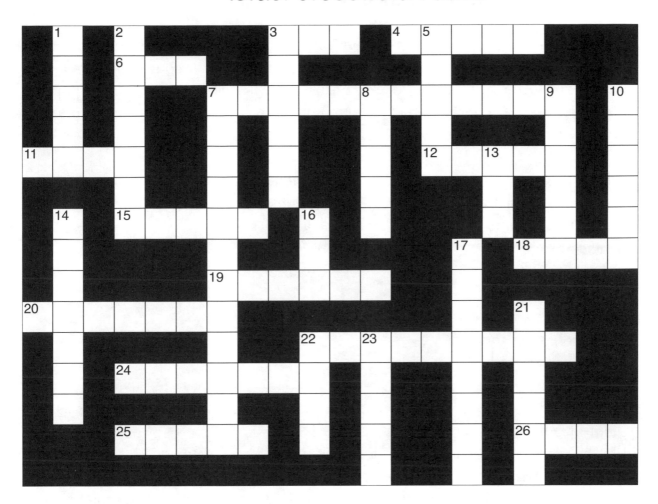

ACROSS

3 Hebrew for "mountain"
4 Israel's neighbor to the south
6 Hebrew word for "mommy"
7 Jerusalem in Hebrew
11 Israel's flag has this in its center
12 In Israel, Jews and _____s must work together for peace
15 Scroll containing the Five Books of Moses
18 The Western _____
19 Israel's flag without the star resembles a _____
20 Settlement where everyone shares equally
22 First prime minister of Israel
24 Fun food in a pita
25 Background color of Israel's flag
26 Hebrew for "spring"; bustling city Tel _____

DOWN

1 City at southern tip of Israel
2 Hebrew name for Sea of Galilee
3 Northern mountain in Israel known for snow
5 Female prime minister of Israel, first name
7 Israeli Independence Day (in Hebrew)
8 Northern port city in Israel
9 Rebels fought to save this desert fortress
10 The Jewish homeland; the State of _____
13 Hebrew word for "daddy"
14 Israel's national anthem
16 Hebrew for "small hill"; bustling city _____ Aviv
17 The Old City of Jerusalem is made up of four of these
21 Like a kibbutz, but you get to own stuff
22 One of Israel's colors
23 Desert in Israel

(see page 74 for answers)

Make Your Own Hummus

Hummus, a favorite Israeli dish, is made out of cooked chickpeas (also called garbanzo beans). It is often served as an appetizer, dip, or first course. In Israel it is usually spread thinly on a salad plate and garnished with olive oil, a dash of paprika, and a sprig of parsley. The Israeli way to eat hummus is to scoop it up with a piece of pita bread. Now you can make your own!

What You'll Need
1 can garbanzo beans, drained
3 T. tahini (ground sesame seeds)
2 T. lemon juice
2½–3 T. olive oil
3 cloves garlic, pressed
salt and pepper, to taste
paprika and parsley for garnish

Utensils
medium bowl
spatula
mixing spoon
food processor

What to Do
1. **Grind** drained garbanzo beans in a food processor until smooth. **Scrape** into a medium-size bowl.
2. **Add** the remaining ingredients and **mix** until the hummus is a spreadable consistency. **Add** water or more lemon juice to thin it.
3. **Serve** in a small bowl or on a salad plate, sprinkled with paprika and garnished with sprigs of parsley. **Accompany** with fresh pita bread. **Keep** refrigerated.

Israel-Lights

Make a wish for Israel on each of the candles and write your wish under each candle on the cake. Then color the cake and the Israel-lights.

HAPPY * B-DAY * ISRAEL

Lag Ba'omer

Lag Ba'omer, the thirty-third day of the counting of the *omer* (a sheaf of barley), is a moment of joy in the fifty-day semi-mourning period between Pesach and Shavuot. On Lag Ba'omer we remember the Jewish teachers and students who, during Roman times, had to teach and study in secret because teaching Torah was forbidden. Rabbi Akiva and Rabbi Shimon bar Yochai continued to teach in secret. Their students would dress up like hunters and carry bows and arrows deep into the woods to study with their teachers. If they were caught by the Romans, they could say they were only hunting. This is why some children today play with toy bows and arrows on Lag Ba'omer. In this chapter you can try to decode your own secret painting, test your skills with a Jewish scholar quiz, and honor your teachers.

Lag Ba'omer Vocabulary

Bar Kochba: Jewish leader who led an unsuccessful revolt against the Romans in the second century C.E.

Lag Ba'omer: The thirty-third day of the counting of the omer

Omer: A measure or sheaf of barley

Rabbi Akiva: Great Jewish teacher who died at the hands of the Romans in the second century C.E.

Rabbi Shimon Bar Yochai: Scholar and mystic during the time of the Bar Kochba Revolt who is said to have died on Lag Ba'omer. Accordng to legend, he spoke out against the Romans and fled to the mountains, hiding out in a cave for twelve years and continuing to teach students secretly.

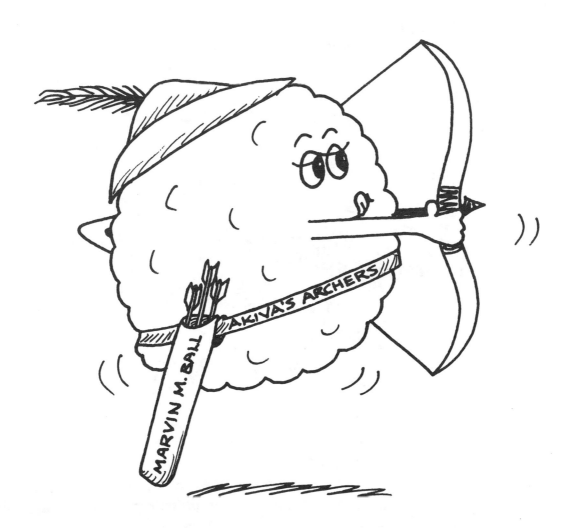

Secret Painting

During Roman times, Rabbi Akiva would teach his students Torah in a hidden cave so that the Romans wouldn't find them. Encode your own secret messages with this easy technique.

What You'll Need

1 white Shabbat candle, with a pointed tip
watercolors
brushes
blank paper

What to Do

1. Using the tip of an unlit candle, **write** in wax on a piece of paper something that would have been forbidden during Rabbi Akiva's time. (HINT: Anything Jewish is a good bet!) You can also write a secret note to a friend, or your Hebrew name. Be creative!
2. To decode the note, **paint over** it with watercolors. The wax from the candle will resist the water, and your secret message will be revealed!

ewish Scholar Quiz

the bows and arrows the students of our rabbis had to
ng in Roman times. To remind us of their courage, your
archer's target. (This is a tough activity. HINT: check out
UAHC Press) and *Chocolate Chip Challah* for help with the

with their most noted teachings and **write** the letter of
ame of the teacher who said it.
ck your answers.

_____ **1.** Rabban Shimon ben Gamliel
_____ **2.** Joshua ben Perachya
_____ **3.** Rabbi Tarfon
_____ **4.** Ben Zoma
_____ **5.** Rashi
kept the _____ **6.** Shammai
Jewish _____ **7.** Hillel
_____ **8.** Rabbi Meir
_____ **9.** Theodore Herzl
we were _____ **10.** Ahad Ha-Am

for me?
? And if

ire for

he work,
it."

n

what it

BLACK

BLUE

RED

CENTER=YELLOW

SCORING:

1–2 correct = black (outer) ring
3–5 correct = blue ring
6–8 correct = red ring
9–10 correct = bull's-eye!
*Draw an arrow in the target
    and try to beat your score!*

peace."

ANSWERS:
1. J   6. A
2. F   7. E
3. G   8. I
4. H   9. B
5. D   10. C

Honor Your Teacher

What to Do

1. **Draw** a picture of your favorite teacher inside the picture frame.
2. **Color** the frame and **add** your own touches to it.
3. **Write** your teacher's name in the blank space at the bottom of the frame.
4. **Write** a blessing for your teacher underneath the picture.

Shavuot

Shavuot, the "Feast of Weeks," began as a harvest festival but has become a time to celebrate the giving of the Torah. It is customary to eat dairy foods and decorate homes and synagogues with flowers, leaves and papercut decorations that celebrate nature's blooming. In this chapter you will get a chance to do an actual papercut, an ancient yet modern art form that is closely tied to Shavuot.

Shavuot Vocabulary

Bikurim: The first fruits or crops of the harvest; usually the first sheaves of wheat brought to the Temple in Jerusalem as a gift to God for a good harvest

Mount Sinai: The mountain in the Sinai desert upon which Moses stood to receive the Ten Commandments

Seven species: Seven species of plants native to the land of Israel that are often mentioned in the Bible, especially in Song of Songs, and that are also mentioned in relation to the harvest: grapes, olives, dates, figs, pomegranates, wheat, and barley

Shavuot: "The Festival of Weeks," a harvest festival coming seven weeks after Pesach, on which we celebrate the harvest and the giving of the Torah

Tikkun: On Shavuot it is customary to have a *Tikkun Leil Shavuot*, during which people stay up all night studying various Jewish texts. It is based on the midrash that when God offered the Ten Commandments to the Jewish people, they weren't ready to receive the Torah, so today we stay up all night studying to show God just how ready we are.

Great Numbers in the Torah Word Search

What to Do

Fill in the blanks using the clues, then find the words in the word search below. Words can be up, down, backwards, forwards, or diagonal.

1. For 40 years the Israelites wandered in the _____.
2. 10 _____ fell upon Egypt.
3. The 7th day of creation is called _____.
4. Pilgrims journeying to Jerusalem brought offerings from the 7 _____.
5. Moses received the 10 _____ on Mount Sinai.
6. The 4 Matriarchs, or Mothers, are Sarah, Rebecca, _____ , and Leah.
7. Jacob's sons became the 12 _____ of Israel.
8. In Joseph's dream, there were eleven _____ in the sky.
9. Abraham, Isaac, and _____ are the 3 Patriarchs, or Fathers.
10. Noah saved at least 2 of every kind of _____.
11. The Ark of the Covenant contained the 2 _____ of the Law.
12. Jacob's 13 children included one daughter, _____.
13. There are five books in the _____.

```
S E A P O K A S E I C E P S X Q A T
O H Q N Y A E U S C U I A K S V F E
L X A B I S I N C O A S L A H E A S
Y R A B O H C A G M M A T N D Y R R
M T G E B H O F A M U E Q A I J M O
A S R J E A V H B A S I K T R A A S
Y P O A E Y T J P N K A A O D S X P
C D D X C L H B A D P B J V S A N T
P A E L I H L A B M L K W O G E A N
I X S F R A E D A E Z Q H A R O T A
H H E M V N A L T N A E I M Y D C L
C Q R O F T S S Y T B N Y E L S T Q
E N T U N O A W A S Z A L T A E A E
B A Z M U R Q A E A L E A U A U B A
O H D T R I B E S E W A M K E G A L
C Y G A A K P A E Y T K I A H A V K
A J O I L U W S M A O Y N D E L K G
J W U P A N I D F E R S A Q R P L A
```

(see answers on page 74)

Shavuot Papercut

A Jewish papercut is *not* what happens when a Jewish kid cuts herself licking an envelope! Papercutting is an ancient art form originating in China and found in many cultures around the world. It involves cutting out intricate designs from a single piece of paper. In Eastern Europe it was customary to decorate the synagogue with papercuts on Shavuot. These tiny snowflake-like designs were called *shavuoslech*, or "little shavuots," in Yiddish. Try the papercut on the following page, then experiment with your own designs. Remember that everything NOT cut out must be connected or it will fall apart.

What You'll Need
a pair of small, sharp-pointed scissors
1 or more pieces of colored construction paper, or tissue paper, or cellophane
glue or glue stick

What to Do
1. **Fold** the paper in half along the dotted line.
2. With the printed side up and using a pair of small, sharp pointed scissors, **cut out** all the shaded areas (the negative space). For the inside areas you will have to **poke** a hole with your scissors to get in. **Cut** slowly and carefully, **turning** the paper around the shapes as you cut.
3. When you're finished cutting out all the shaded areas, carefully **unfold** the papercut and **flatten** out the creases with your fingers.
4. The side with no printing on it is the front. Now **decide** what color background you would like.
5. FOR SINGLE COLOR BACKGROUND: **Flip over** the papercut so the printed side is face up. **Apply** a small amount of glue or glue stick to the back side, then, holding it by the edges, **place** it carefully right side up onto your background piece. **Smooth out** the papercut, going from the creases out.
6. FOR MULTICOLORED BACKGROUND: **Place** the papercut face down on the table (printed side facing you). **Glue** different colored pieces of construction or tissue paper behind the different sections of the papercut. If you use tissue paper or cellophane, you can put the papercut in the window and have a light catcher. Make sure you **turn** it **over** and **trim** any excess paper from the edges.

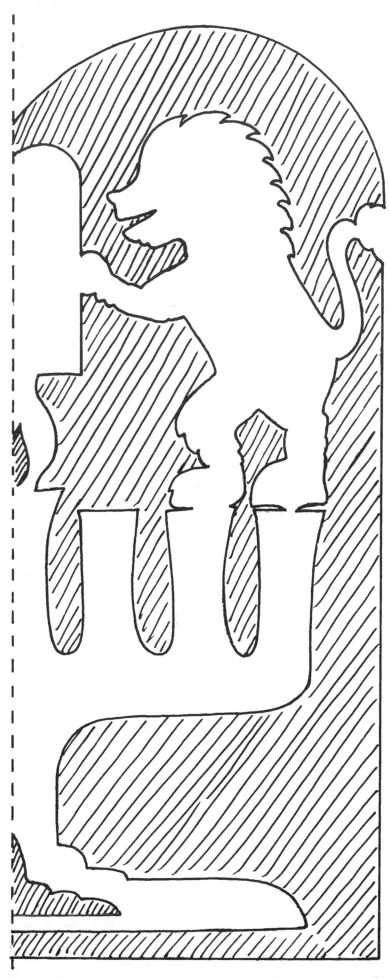

Tishah B'av

Tishah B'av, the ninth (*tishah*) day of the month Av, is a solemn day in the Jewish year. Tishah B'av marks the day when both the First and Second Temples in Jerusalem were destroyed and the people Israel began their exile. Tishah B'av is also viewed as a day when other tragedies have befallen the Jewish people. Because Tishah B'av is a day of sadness, some Jews fast and refrain from doing certain activities, just as on Yom Kippur. It is also a tradition to read and study books that are in keeping with the solemn mood of the day. Despite these tragedies, the Jewish people have not only survived, but thrived. In this chapter you will be able to make a decorative *yizkor* candle and create a puzzle of the Temple to see what it might have looked like before it was destroyed.

Tishah B'av Vocabulary

Babylonia: The country to which the Jews were expelled from Jerusalem and in which they began their exile

First Temple: The First Temple in Jerusalem, a grand palace where Jews from all over came to offer sacrifices, built by King Solomon and destroyed in 586 B.C.E. by the Babylonian King Nebuchadnezzar

Kotel: The "Western Wall" in the Old City of Jerusalem, the last remaining piece of the retaining wall of the platform upon which stood the Second Temple

Second Temple: The Second Temple in Jerusalem, built by King Herod during the Roman period, even larger and grander than the first; destroyed by the Roman Emperor Titus in 70 C.E., exactly 656 years to the day after the First Temple was destroyed, according to legend

Tishah B'av: The ninth day of the month of Av, a solemn day marking the day on which the First and Second Temples in Jerusalem were both destroyed and the people Israel began their exile

Decorative Yizkor Candle

A *yizkor* candle is lit as a memorial for someone close to us who has died. We light a *yizkor* candle on Tishah B'av to remember the destruction of the Temples in Jerusalem. This activity gives you a chance to decorate a *yizkor* candleholder and make it more than just a plain glass. This activity can also be used for Yom Kippur.

What You'll Need
a glass yizkor candleholder
a sheet of white tissue paper
pieces of assorted colored tissue paper
scissors
markers or colored pencils
glue stick

What to Do
1. **Run** the glass under warm to hot tap water to **remove** the label.
2. **Cut** a piece of white tissue paper to fit around your candle, (4 x 8 inches for most glass yizkor candles)
3. **Cut** or **tear** pieces of colored tissue paper and **make** a collage on the white strip of tissue, **gluing** the pieces down with a glue stick. **Experiment** with layering different shapes to create varying shades.
4. Use markers or colored pencils to **write** someone's name on the strip, or the word YIZKOR ("remember"). Here is how to write it in Hebrew:

5. Now put glue on the back of the strip and **glue** the tissue around the glass. Watch the reflections and the colors change as the candle burns.

Second Temple Puzzle

Cut along outside edge and **paste** or **glue** puzzle onto oak tag, a manilla folder or thin cardboard.

Cut apart the puzzle pieces with scissors or an Xacto knife (DO THIS WITH AN ADULT), and **put** the Second Temple **back together** again. Keep pieces in a ziploc bag.

Rosh Chodesh

Rosh Chodesh celebrates the appearance of the new moon and the beginning of a new month in the Jewish calendar. The Jewish calendar is based on a lunar cycle—the amount of time it takes the moon to orbit the Earth—twenty-nine and one-half days. Rosh Chodesh is celebrated for one or two days, depending on the length of the previous month. In this chapter you will make a cookie jar to hold the Woman in the Moon Cookies from the *Chocolate Chip Challah* cookbook.

Rosh Chodesh Vocabulary

Lunar cycle: The twenty-nine and one-half days it takes the moon to orbit the earth; the cycle on which the Jewish calendar is based

New moon: The phase of the moon when nothing is visible in the sky, to when the moon is just barely a sliver; the beginning of the lunar cycle

Rosh Chodesh: The celebration of the new moon, a time traditionally celebrated by women and being reclaimed today by them as a time to study, sing, and celebrate together

Hebrew Months Matching Game

Trying *not* to use your compass from the Rosh haShanah chapter, draw a line to match up the Hebrew months with their corresponding holidays.

TISHREI   Pesach, Yom haShoah

KISLEV   Purim

SHEVAT   Yom haAtzmaut, Lag Ba'omer

ADAR   Tishah B'av

PURIM   Shavuot

NISAN   Rosh haShanah, Yom Kippur, Sukot, Simchat Torah

IYAR

SIVAN   Chanukah

                      Tu Bishvat

AV

Answers: Tishrei=Rosh haShanah, Yom Kippur, Sukot…; Kislev=Chanukah; Shevat=Tu Bishvat; Adar=Purim; Nisan=Pesach, Yom haShoah; Iyar=Yom haAtzmaut, Lag Ba'omer; Sivan=Shavuot; Av=Tishah B'av.

Woman in the Moon Cookie Jar

Make this jar to hold your Woman in the Moon Cookies.

What You'll Need
a coffee can or other can or jar with lid, big enough for cookies
a sheet of white paper large enough to wrap around the can
colored crayons
watercolors and brush
glue or glue stick

What to Do
1. **Measure** a strip of paper to fit around your coffee can or jar. With colored crayons, **draw** a picture of the different phases of the moon, a sky filled with stars, a woman in the moon for Rosh Chodesh, or any other appropriate design that comes to mind.
2. **Take** your watercolors and, using a dark color like deep blue, black, or purple, **paint** over the picture you just drew. The watercolors will resist the crayon, and you will have a beautiful color-resist painting.
3. When it's all dry, **wrap** your painting around the jar and **glue** the ends together. **Trim off** the excess paper. You now have a Woman in the Moon Cookie Jar!

Tu Bishvat Word Search Answers

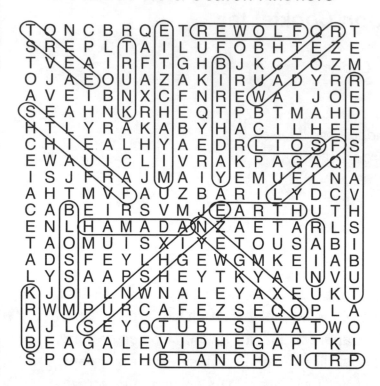

Purim Crossword Puzzle Answers

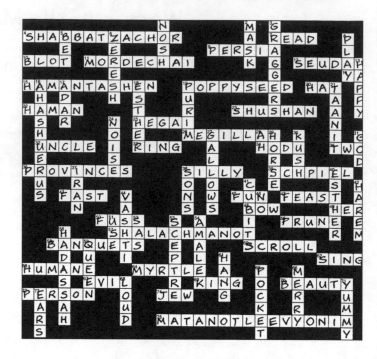

Israel Crossword Puzzle Answers

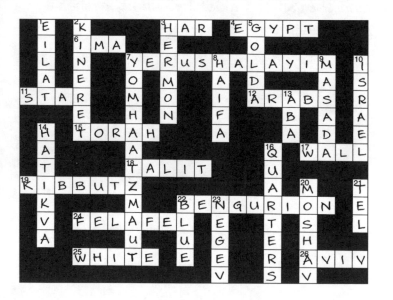

Great Numbers
Word Search Answers

1. DESERT
2. PLAGUES
3. SHABBAT
4. SPECIES
5. COMMANDMENTS
6. RACHEL
7. TRIBES
8. STARS
9. JACOB
10. ANIMAL
11. TABLETS
12. DINA
13. TORAH

אבגדהוזחטי
כךלמםנןסע
פףצץקרשת

אבגדההוזחטי
כךלממנןסע
פףצץקרשת

שַׁבָּת שָׁלוֹם